Comparing Past and Present

Playing with Friends

Rebecca Rissman

Heinemann
LIBRARY

Chicago, Illinois

© 2014 Heinemann Library
an imprint of Capstone Global Library, LLC
Chicago, Illinois

To contact Capstone Global Library please phone 800-747-4992, or visit our website www.capstonepub.com

Edited by Rebecca Rissman, Daniel Nunn, and
   Catherine Veitch
Designed by Philippa Jenkins
Picture research by Elizabeth Alexander
Production by Helen McCreath
Originated by Capstone Global Library Ltd

Library of Congress Cataloging-in-Publication Data
Rissman, Rebecca.
  Playing with friends / Rebecca Rissman.—First edition.
     pages cm.—(Comparing past and present)
  Includes bibliographical references and index.
  ISBN 978-1-4329-8993-4 (hb)—ISBN 978-1-4329-9027-5 (pb)
1. Play—History. 2. Games—History. 3. Play—History. 4. Sports—History. I. Title.
  GV1201 .R54 2013
  649'.5—dc23   2013012546

Acknowledgments
We would like to thank the following for permission to reproduce photographs: Alamy: Asia Images Group LLC, 15, Kuttig - People, 9, 23; Getty Images: Fox Photos, 4, 14, FPG/Staff, 20, Fuse, 11, H. Armstrong Roberts, cover (right), Harold M. Lambert, 8, 22, 23, Hulton-Deutsch Collection, 6, 18, 23, Martin Barraud, 19, Richards, 10, 23, Tanya Constantine, cover (left), Vintage Images, 12, Westend61, 21; Shutterstock: Blend Images, 7, Golden Pixels LLC, 13; Superstock: 4X5 Collection/Devaney, back cover, 16, Cultura Limited, 17, marka/marco albonico/Marka, 5

We would like to thank Nancy Harris and Diana Bentley for their invaluable help in the preparation of this book.

Contents

Comparing the Past and Present 4

Games 8

Entertainment 10

Playing Outdoors 12

Toys 16

Friends Far Away 20

Then and Now 22

Picture Glossary 23

Index 24

Note to Parents and Teachers 24

Comparing the Past and Present

Things in the past have already happened.

Things in the present are happening now.

Playing with friends has changed over time.

The way children play with friends today is very different from the past.

Games

In the past, children played simple games. Some children played marbles.

Today, some children play
computer games.

Entertainment

In the past, children listened to stories on the radio.

Today, many children watch television.

Playing Outdoors

In the past, children swam in rivers or lakes.

Always swim with an adult.

Today, most children swim in swimming pools.

In the past, some children wore roller skates.

Today, many children wear
roller blades.

Toys

metal

In the past, most children's toys were made of metal or wood.

plastic

Today, most children's toys are made of plastic.

17

In the past, many toys were handmade.

Today, most toys are made by machines in factories.

Friends Far Away

In the past, some children wrote letters to friends who lived far away.

Today, some children use a computer to talk to friends who live far away.

Then and Now

In the past, children played jump rope with their friends. Today, children

still play jump rope!

Picture Glossary

 **computer games** electronic games played on a computer or TV

 **handmade** something that is made by a person and not by a machine

 **marbles** small glass toys that are rolled in a simple game

 **radio** machine that plays music and stories. It also plays news.

Index

computers 9, 21, 23

jump rope 22

letters 20

marbles 8, 23

radio 10, 23

roller blades 15

roller skates 14

swimming 12, 13

television 11

toys 16, 17, 18, 19

Note to Parents and Teachers

Before reading

Talk to children about the difference between the past and present. Explain that the word *past* refers to things that have already happened. The word *present* refers to things that are happening now. Ask children to describe what they did yesterday or earlier in the day, and then explain that those activities took place in the past.

After reading

- Explain that the way children played with their friends has changed over time. Ask children to name their favorite things to do with their friends. Make a list of the activities on the board. Then, go down the list and tell children which activities would not have been possible in the past.

- Turn to pages 8—9 and explain that technology has changed the way children play over time.

- Encourage children to think of activities they enjoy doing with their friends today that would have been similar in the past. For example, jump rope and playing hide-and-seek are activities that have changed very little over time.